"Study to show thyself approved unto God, a workman that needs not to be ashamed."
2nd Timothy 2:15

CALLED

TO

MINISTRY

A Practical Study Guide of Subjects that are
Essential for Ministry Preparation

Dr. S. Walker

TABLE OF CONTENTS

From the moment we commit our lives to Christ we have an inherent desire to give something back. The reason for this is our deep appreciation of His atoning sacrifice that put us in fellowship with God our Father.

The wonderful truth is that we can. Because of our regeneration, we have all been endowed with Spiritual Gifts. And, some of us will realize that we have been set apart as Ministry Gifts to The Body of Christ.

"Called to Ministry" is a practical study of subjects and protocols that are essential for ministry preparation. Written in an easy to read format, this study manual will give you the clarity and understanding you need to fulfill the burning desire in your heart to give something back to Christ … "yourself."

"Study to show thyself approved unto God,
a workman that needs not to be ashamed."
2nd Timothy 2:15

Dedicated to Caleb Paul Georg

*"And Caleb stilled the people before Moses, and said,
Let us go up at once, and possess it; for we are well
able to overcome it." Numbers 13:30*

CHAPTER ONE

SEVEN KEYS TO GOOD LEADERSHIP

KEY #1: BE AN EXAMPLE

Every good leader should realize that they are being carefully watched by everyone. That is why it is important that they set themselves as an example to be followed. This is effectively done by practicing what they teach and preach through their personal lifestyles.

2nd Timothy 1:12-13 "For this reason I also suffer these things, but I am not ashamed; for I know whom I have believed and I am convinced that He is able to guard what I have entrusted to Him until that day. Retain the standard of sound words which you have heard from me, in the faith and love which are in Christ Jesus."

KEY #2: EDUCATION

Leaders should not expect to be proficient in their ministries without educating themselves. Leadership education should *include:*

- Seminary training
- Attending seminars and workshops in their specific field of ministry
- Extensive reading both personal and ministry related
- Being knowledgeable of current events

2nd Timothy 4:2 "Preach the word; be instant in season, out of season; reprove, rebuke, exhort with all longsuffering and doctrine."

2nd Timothy 2:15 "Study to shew thyself approved unto God, a workman that needeth not to be ashamed, rightly dividing the word of truth."

KEY #3: SOBRIETY

Friendliness and being approachable are excellent characteristics of a good leader. People are drawn to a warm, friendly yet serious leader. However, familiarity, folly and foolish gesturing compromises respect.

Ephesians 5:2 "And walk in love, as Christ also hath loved us, and hath given himself for us an offering and a sacrifice to God for a sweetsmelling savour."

Titus 2:7 "In all things shewing thyself a pattern of good works: in doctrine shewing uncorruptness, gravity, sincerity."

KEY #4: TRUST

While working closely with people, a leader can expect that personal issues and secrets will be shared in a counseling session or specific request for prayer. It is therefore, imperative that a leader be trustworthy. A good leader will never breach someone's confidence in them.

Proverbs 11:13 "Whoever spreads gossip betrays secrets, but the trustworthy person keeps a confidence." International Standard Version

KEY #5: GIFTS AND TALENTS

Scripture explains that there are different "Spiritual Gifts" and talents given to each member of the Body of Christ. One of the most important responsibilities of a good leader is to help those in their care to notice and use their gifts.

2nd Timothy 1:5-6 "When I call to remembrance the unfeigned faith that is in thee, which dwelt first in thy grandmother Lois, and thy mother Eunice; and I am persuaded that in thee also. Wherefore I put thee in remembrance that thou stir up the gift of God, which is in thee by the putting on of my hands."

KEY #6: MOTIVATE

We have already said that each member of the Body of Christ has one or more "Spiritual Gift" and talents with enough faith to operate them. A good leader will encourage and motivate individuals to practice their gifts so as to enhance them.

Good leadership skills include the willingness to train and motivate others. There are three basic principles to accomplishing *this:*

- Always make very clear what you want accomplished
- Evaluate the person's competence and their ability to complete the task
- Identify specific areas you need to concentrate on in your training of the person

2ⁿᵈ Timothy 4:2 "Preach the word; be instant in season, out of season; reprove, rebuke, exhort with all longsuffering and doctrine."

KEY #7: DELEGATION

Although a leader is ultimately responsible for the success or failure of their ministry, they are not required to work in ministry alone. A good leader understands this and is willing to delegate some of the responsibilities of ministry. Entrusting others and sharing responsibilities lessens the strain of ministry, which leads to its growth and expansion.

Titus 1:4-5 "To Titus, mine own son after the common faith: Grace, mercy, and peace, from God the Father and the Lord Jesus Christ our Saviour. For this cause left I thee in Crete, that thou shouldest set in order the things that are wanting, and ordain elders in every city, as I had appointed thee."

NOTES

NOTES

CALLED TO LEADERSHIP WORKSHEET
EXAMPLES TO LEARN FROM

Abraham – *Genesis 12:1* "Now the LORD had said unto Abram, Get thee out of thy country, and from thy kindred, and from thy father's house, unto a land that I will shew thee."

Observation: _____

Mistake(s) we shouldn't make:

_____

_____

Moses – *Exodus 3:10-11* "Come now therefore, and I will send thee unto Pharaoh, that thou mayest bring forth my people the children of Israel out of Egypt. And Moses said unto God, Who am I, that I should go unto Pharaoh, and that I should bring forth the children of Israel out of Egypt?"

Observation: _____

Mistake(s) we shouldn't make:

_____

_____

Gideon – *Judges 6:14-15* "And the LORD looked upon him, and said, Go in this thy might, and thou shalt save Israel from the hand of the Midianites: have not I sent thee? And he said unto him, Oh my Lord, wherewith shall I save Israel? behold, my family is poor in Manasseh, and I am the least in my father's house."

Observation: _____

Mistake(s) we shouldn't make:

_____

_____

Elisha and Elijah – *1ˢᵗ Kings 19:19-20* "So he departed from there and found Elisha the son of Shaphat, while he was plowing with twelve pairs of oxen before him, and he with the twelfth. And Elijah passed over to him and threw his mantle on him. He left the oxen and ran after Elijah and said, "Please let me kiss my father and my mother, then I will follow you." And he said to him, "Go back again, for what have I done to you?" New American Standard Version

Observation: _____

Mistake(s) we shouldn't make:

_____

_____

Read the following Scripture and apply it to your own life:

Isaiah 6:1-8 "In the year of King Uzziah's death I saw the Lord sitting on a throne, lofty and exalted, with the train of His robe filling the temple. Seraphim stood above Him, each having six wings: with two he covered his face, and with two he covered his feet, and with two he flew. And one called out to another and said, "Holy, Holy, Holy, is the LORD of hosts, The whole earth is full of His glory." And the foundations of the thresholds trembled at the voice of him who called out, while the temple was filling with smoke. Then I said, "Woe is me, for I am ruined! Because I am a man of unclean lips, And I live among a people of unclean lips; For my eyes have seen the King, the LORD of hosts." Then one of the seraphim flew to me with a burning coal in his hand, which he had taken from the altar with tongs. He touched my mouth with it and said, "Behold, this has touched your lips; and your iniquity is taken away and your sin is forgiven." Then I heard the voice of the Lord, saying, "Whom shall I send, and who will go for Us?" Then I said, "Here am I. Send me!" New International Version

CHAPTER TWO

SEEKING THE WILL OF GOD

Definition:

To *"will"* is to wish or purpose to carry out, to decide upon, bring about to purpose, elect, one's pleasure, disposition, decision.

God has a plan and purpose for each of our lives. It is revealed to us through His Will, which makes knowing His Will a personal responsibility.

Colossians 1:9-11 "For this cause we also, since the day we heard *it*, do not cease to pray for you, and to desire that ye might be filled with the knowledge of his will in all wisdom and spiritual understanding; That ye might walk worthy of the Lord unto all pleasing, being fruitful in every good work, and increasing in the knowledge of God; Strengthened with all might, according to his glorious power, unto all patience and longsuffering with joyful-ness."

SEEKING GOD

Seeking is the most effective way to discover what God's specific Will is for our personal lives as well as our Christian service. However, there are fundamentals of God's Will that we must seek for first. *We should first seek for:*

THE HOUSE OF THE LORD

In *2nd Chronicles 6:2*, Solomon's Temple was referred to as "The Habitation of God." The church in the New Testament is "The Habitation of God in the Spirit." In both of the Testaments, it is where we go to be in the presence of God, His house ... His Habitation. We should therefore, try to have the same spiritual desire David had, which was to go into God's House consistently to receive spiritual vision and understanding of His Will for our lives.

Psalm 27:4 "One thing have I desired of the LORD, that will I seek after; that I may dwell in the house of the LORD all the days of my life, to behold the beauty of the LORD, and to inquire in his temple."

THE THINGS PERTAINING TO GOD'S KINGDOM

Luke Chapter 12 gives us examples of the way we perceive bless-ings, which are mainly focused on provisions for the cares of life. Unfortunately, these blessings are temporal. We should rather seek for more of the things that are spiritual as a priority. Everything else that we need will be provided for us if we do. This is a promise from God.

Luke 12:31 "But rather seek ye the kingdom of God; and all these things shall be added unto you."

THINGS ABOVE

Being spiritually resurrected in Christ, we should affectionately set our minds on heavenly things.

Colossians 3:1-2 "If ye then be risen with Christ, seek those things which are above, where Christ sitteth on the right hand of God. Set your affection on things above, not on things on the earth."

WE SHOULD SEEK GOD

WITH PASSION – WITH OUR HEARTS AND SOULS

Heart and Soul are used interchangeable in Scripture and refers to the center of our emotions. Therefore, when we attempt to seek God's Will, we are to do it passionately, fervently and enthusiasti-cally.

Deuteronomy 4:29 "But if from there you seek the LORD your God, you will find him if you seek him with all your heart and with all your soul."

BY TEARING DOWN THE "GROVES" IN OUR LIVES

Groves in Scripture consisted of idols, monuments or shrines that were objects of heathenistic worship. Applied personally, groves of the heart are the things we adore to the point that they can distract us from our worship and service to God.

2ⁿᵈ Chronicles 19:3 "Nevertheless there are good things found in you, in that you have taken away the groves out of the land, and have prepared your heart to seek God." American King James Version

WHEN SHOULD WE SEEK GOD

We should seek God early, before we become dry and have lost our zeal. Knowing God's Will for our lives is refreshing; it strengthens us and helps us to grow.

Psalm 63:1-2 "A Psalm of David, when he was in the wilderness of Judah. O God, thou *art* my God; early will I seek thee: my soul thirsteth for thee, my flesh longeth for thee in a dry and thirsty land, where no water is; to see thy power and thy glory, so *as* I have seen thee in the sanctuary."

THE RESULTS OF KNOWING GOD'S WILL

REWARDS

Hebrew 11:6 "But without faith *it is* impossible to please *him*: for he that cometh to God must believe that he is, and *that* he is a rewarder of them that diligently seek him."

JOY AND GLADNESS

Psalm 69:32 "The humble shall see *this, and* be glad: and your heart shall live that seek God."

Psalm 22:26 "The meek shall eat and be satisfied: they shall praise the LORD that seek him: your heart shall live forever."

EXPERIENCE OF GOD'S GOODNESS

Lamentations 3:25 "The LORD *is* good unto them that wait for him, to the soul *that* seeketh him."

ASSURANCE OF HIS PRESENCE

Psalm 9:10 "And they that know thy name will put their trust in thee: for thou, LORD, hast not forsaken them that seek thee."

Psalm 27:7-9 "Hear, O LORD, when I cry with my voice: have mercy also upon me, and answer me. When thou saidst, Seek ye my face; my heart said unto thee, Thy face, LORD, will I seek. Hide not thy face far from me; put not thy servant away in anger: thou hast been my help; leave me not, neither forsake me, O God of my salvation."

SEVEN SPIRITUAL POSITIONS TO BE IN TO KNOW GOD'S WILL

1. **SUBMISSION** – to be obedient, to comply with or given in to. In other words we must stop resisting and simply give in to God's Will for our lives.

   Philippians 2:12-13 "Wherefore, my beloved, as ye have always obeyed, not as in my presence only, but now much more in my absence, work out your own salvation with fear and trembling. For it is God which worketh in you both to will and to do of his good pleasure."

2. **PRUDENCE** – to walk up-right or cautiously and not fool-ishly. It means to be serious about spiritual things. When seeking the Will of God, sometimes separation is necessary.

   Ephesians 5:16-17 "Redeeming the time, because the days are evil. Wherefore be ye not unwise, but understanding what the will of the Lord is."

3. **CONSECRATION**

   Romans 12:1-2 "I beseech you therefore, brethren, by the mercies of God, that ye present your bodies a living sacrifice, holy, acceptable unto God, which is your reasonable service. And be not conformed to this world: but be ye transformed by the renewing of your mind, that ye may prove what is that good, and acceptable, and perfect, will of God."

4. **AWARENESS OF THE VOICE OF GOD** – is to positively distinguish the difference *between:*

    - our own thinking or opinion
    - Satan's influence
    - the leading, insight and direction of God

    John 10:5 "And a stranger will they not follow, but will flee from him: for they know not the voice of strangers."

5. **MATURITY** – the knowledge of God's Will requires a strong desire to grow and become stronger in faith, actions and deeds.

    Hebrews 13:20-21 "Now the God of peace, that brought again from the dead our Lord Jesus, that great shepherd of the sheep, through the blood of the everlasting covenant, Make you perfect in every good work to do his will, working in you that which is well pleasing in his sight, through Jesus Christ; to whom be glory for ever and ever. Amen."

    1ˢᵗ Peter 2:2 "As newborn babes, desire the sincere milk of the word, that ye may grow thereby."

6. **FELLOWSHIP AND INTIMACY WITH GOD** – trough prayer, meditation, worship and study of the Word are significant ways of spending time with the Father.

    Luke 6:12 "And it came to pass in those days, that he went out into a mountain to pray, and continued all night in prayer to God."

7. **BEING SENSITIVE TO THE LEADING OF THE HOLY SPIRIT** – is to be responsive, receptive or to have an awareness of how the Holy Spirit is directing us.

    Acts 16:6-9 "Now when they had gone throughout Phrygia and the region of Galatia, and were forbidden of the Holy Ghost to preach the word in Asia, after they were come to

Mysia, they assayed to go into Bithynia: but the Spirit suffered them not. And they passing by Mysia, came down to Troas. And a vision appeared to Paul in the night; there stood a man of Macedonia, and prayed him, saying, 'Come over into Macedonia, and help us.'"

There are two actions that must be taken after gaining the knowledge of God's Will:

First, we must bring our own will into subjection to God's Will.

Matthew 26:39 "And he went a little further, and fell on his face, and prayed, saying, O my Father, if it be possible, let this cup pass from me: nevertheless not as I will, but as thou *wilt.*"

John 6:38 "For I came down from heaven, not to do mine own will, but the will of him that sent me."

Second, we must be diligent to perform the Will of God.

Psalm 40:8 "I delight to do thy will, O my God: yea, thy law *is* within my heart."

NOTES

NOTES

Seeking the Will of God Worksheet

Identify the "Groves" in your life and how you intend to bring them down.

_____

_____

_____

_____

_____

_____

_____

_____

_____

_____

_____

_____

_____

_____

_____

_____

_____

_____

_____

_____

_____

_____

CHAPTER THREE

AN EXPLANATION OF THE ANOINTING

FOUR METHODS OF THE ANOINTING

You can be anointed *by:*

SOMEONE ELSE TO HONOR YOU

John 11:2 "Mary was the woman who anointed the Lord with perfume and wiped his feet with her hair. Her brother Lazarus was the one who was ill." New American Standard

A PASTOR OR GROUP OF ELDERS TO PLACE YOU IN A MINISTRY OFFICE

1ˢᵗ Samuel 10:1 "Then Samuel took a flask of olive oil and poured it on Saul's head and kissed him, saying, 'Has not the LORD anointed you ruler over his inheritance?'"

1ˢᵗ Samuel 16:12-13 "And he sent, and brought him in. Now he was ruddy, and withal of a beautiful countenance, and goodly to look to. And the LORD said, Arise, anoint him: for this is he. Then Samuel took the horn of oil, and anointed him in the midst of his brethren: and the Spirit of the LORD came upon David from that day forward. So Samuel rose up, and went to Ramah."

YOURSELF AS A MEANS OF CONSECRATION

Ruth 3:3 "Wash thyself therefore, and anoint thee, and put thy raiment upon thee, and get thee down to the floor: *but* make not thyself known unto the man, until he shall have done eating and drinking."

Matthew 6:17-18 "But thou, when thou fastest, anoint thine head, and wash thy face; That thou appear not unto men to fast, but unto thy Father which is in secret: and thy Father, which seeth in secret, shall reward thee openly."

GOD

2ⁿᵈ Corinthians 1:21-22 "Now it is God who makes both us and you stand firm in Christ. He anointed us, set his seal of ownership on us, and put his Spirit in our hearts as a deposit, guaranteeing what is to come." New International Version

THREE ASPECTS OF THE ANOINTING

CEREMONIAL ANOINTING – a ritual performed when placing a person into a Ministry Office.

1ˢᵗ Kings 19:16 "And Jehu the son of Nimshi you shall anoint king over Israel; and Elisha the son of Shaphat of Abel-meholah you shall anoint as prophet in your place." New American Standard Version

SYMBOLIC ANOINTING by The Holy Spirit for Sanctification

Mark 1:8 "I baptized you in water; But he shall baptize you in the Holy Spirit." American Standard Version

BEING ANOINTED BY THE HOLY SPIRIT – we learn the following as it relates to being Anointed by the *Holy Spirit:*

1. The anointing of the Holy Spirit keeps the believer wise, sober, intelligent and resistant to false doctrine.

   1ˢᵗ John 2:27 "But the anointing which ye have received of him abideth in you, and ye need not that any man teach you: but as the same anointing teacheth you of all things, and is truth, and is no lie, and even as it hath taught you, ye shall abide in him."

2. Just as Jesus was anointed by the baptism of the Holy Spirit for power, so should every believer.

   Isaiah 61:1 "The Spirit of the Lord GOD *is* upon me; because the LORD hath anointed me to preach good tidings unto the meek; he hath sent me to bind up the broken-hearted, to proclaim liberty to the captives, and the opening of the prison to *them that are* bound."

   Acts 10:38 "How God anointed Jesus of Nazareth with the Holy Ghost and with power: who went about doing good,

31

and healing all that were oppressed of the devil; for God was with him."

2nd Timothy 1:7 "For God hath not given us the spirit of fear; but of power, and of love, and of a sound mind."

Luke 24:49 "And, behold, I send the promise of my Father upon you: but tarry ye in the city of Jerusalem, until ye be endued with power from on high."

Acts 1:8 "But ye shall receive power, after that the Holy Ghost is come upon you: and ye shall be witnesses unto me both in Jerusalem, and in all Judaea, and in Samaria, and unto the uttermost part of the earth."

3. The anointing of the Holy Spirit gives Godly power; if there is no power, there is no anointing.

Acts 8:17-2 "Then they began laying their hands on them, and they were receiving the Holy Spirit. Now when Simon saw that the Spirit was bestowed through the laying on of the apostles' hands, he offered them money, saying, "Give this authority to me as well, so that everyone on whom I lay my hands may receive the Holy Spirit." But Peter said to him, "May your silver perish with you, because you thought you could obtain the gift of God with money!'"

Scripture shows us that a person can lose their Spiritual anointing.

1st Samuel 15:22-23 "And Samuel said, Hath the LORD as great delight in burnt offerings and sacrifices, as in obeying the voice of the LORD? Behold, to obey is better than sacrifice, and to hearken than the fat of rams. For rebellion is as the sin of witchcraft, and stubbornness is as iniquity and idolatry. Because thou hast rejected the word of the LORD, he hath also rejected thee from being king."

1st Samuel 16:23 "And it came to pass, when the evil spirit from God was upon Saul, that David took an harp, and played with his hand: so Saul was refreshed, and was well, and the evil spirit departed from him."

The Anointing by the Holy Spirit cannot be passed from one person to another, because of these *two reasons:*

First: It is a Divine bestowal

Second: It is particular to each individual

John 14:12 "I tell you the truth, anyone who believes in me will do the same works I have done, and even greater works, because I am going to be with the Father." New Living Translation

Clarification of the misunderstanding of 2nd Kings 2:9-10

"And it came to pass, when they were gone over, that Elijah said unto Elisha, Ask what I shall do for thee, before I be taken away from thee. And Elisha said, I pray thee, let a double portion of thy spirit be upon me. And he said, Thou hast asked a hard thing: nevertheless, if thou see me when I am taken from thee, it shall be so unto thee; but if not, it shall not be so."

1. Elijah knew he was leaving to be with God and wanted to bless his student or "son in the ministry."

2. Elisha requested a *"double portion"* of Elijah's spirit not his anointing. He was referring to the Law of Moses which states that the firstborn son was entitled to receive twice the inheritance of his father's other sons and the right to be his successor. The first born was given a double portion of all that his father had because he was the first fruit of his strength.

   Therefore, as Elijah's "son in the ministry" *(which was a relationship not shared by the other students)*; Elisha, asked for his spiritual inheritance.

Deuteronomy 21:17 "But he shall acknowledge the son of the hated *for* the firstborn, by giving him a double portion of all that he hath: for he *is* the beginning of his strength; the right of the firstborn *is* his."

3. The request was hard for Elijah to grant because it was up to Elisha to learn from and understand what was going to happen supernaturally. He also had to be ready to use what he learned from that lesson in his own ministry.

We all duplicate *(in one way or another)* the ability, wisdom and characteristics of our parents, teachers, elders or spiritual mentors. We think like them in some ways as well and, can sometimes hear ourselves speaking like them. If we are around an influential person for a long period of time and allow them to impart into our lives, we will pick-up some of their personality, mannerisms and strengths, thus receiving their spirit...who they are.

Elisha proved to be a good "son in the ministry" of Elijah, by using the mantel in the same way his mentor did.

2nd Kings 2:14-15 "And he took the mantle of Elijah that fell from him, and smote the waters, and said, where is the LORD God of Elijah? And when he also had smitten the waters, they parted hither and thither: and Elisha went over. And when the sons of the prophets which were to view at Jericho saw him, they said, The spirit of Elijah doth rest on Elisha. And they came to meet him, and bowed themselves to the ground before him."

OTHER IMPORTANT BENEFITS OF THE ANOINTING

We have learned how important the anointing is for the call to ministry and the performance of its duties. But, the anointing also provides the believer with power and strength to destroy the spiritual yokes *(burdens and bondages)* of the adversary.

1st Samuel 2:10 "The adversaries of the LORD shall be broken to pieces; out of heaven shall he thunder upon them: the LORD shall judge the ends of the earth; and he shall give strength unto his king, and exalt the horn of his anointed."

Psalm 92:10 "But my horn shalt thou exalt like *the horn of* an unicorn: I shall be anointed with fresh oil."

Isaiah 10:27 "And it shall come to pass in that day, *that* his burden shall be taken away from off thy shoulder, and his yoke from off thy neck, and the yoke shall be destroyed because of the anointing."

NOTES

NOTES

AN EXPLANATION OF THE ANOINTING WORKSHEET

Do you feel that you are anointed? Explain your answer.

_____

_____

_____

_____

_____

_____

_____

What are some of the proofs that you have of your anointing.

_____

_____

_____

_____

Is the anointing on your life recognizable by other people? Explain how.

_____

_____

_____

_____

_____

_____

_____

_____

_____

CHAPTER FOUR

INTRODUCTION TO SPIRITUAL GIFTS

A study of the Corinthian Church gives us the background for the main purpose of Spiritual Gifts and their proper use. This background shows us *the:*

FOUNDATION

The foundation for receiving and utilizing Spiritual Gifts is the acceptance of the Lordship of Jesus Christ.

1st Corinthians 12:1-3 "Now concerning spiritual *gifts*, brethren, I would not have you ignorant. Ye know that ye were Gentiles, carried away unto these dumb idols, even as ye were led. Wherefore I give you to understand, that no man speaking by the Spirit of God calleth Jesus accursed: and *that* no man can say that Jesus is the Lord, but by the Holy Ghost."

VARIETIES

There are varieties of Spiritual Gifts that, although they may operate differently, are from the same Lord and authenticated by one God.

1st Corinthians 12:4-7 "Now there are diversities of *gifts*, but the same Spirit. And there are differences of administrations, but the same Lord. And there are diversities of operations, but it is the same God which worketh all in all. But the manifestation of the Spirit is given to every man to profit withal."

GIFTS

The Nine Spiritual Gifts bestowed upon believers as the Holy Spiritual wills *(when He wants you to operate either of these gifts)* are the Word of Wisdom, Word of Knowledge, Faith, Healing, Working of Miracles, Prophecy, Discerning of Spirits, Diversity of Tongues and the Interpretation of Tongues. These *gifts* are not exclusive to one individual and more than one *gift* may be given.

1st Corinthians 12:8-11 "For to one is given by the Spirit the word of wisdom; to another the word of knowledge by the same Spirit; To another faith by the same Spirit; to another the gifts of healing by the same Spirit; To another the working of miracles; to another prophecy; to another discerning of spirits; to another divers kinds of tongues; to another the interpretation of tongues: But all these worketh that one and the selfsame Spirit, dividing to every man severally as he will." Read Romans 12:3-8

UNIFICATION FACTOR

There is no bias when it comes to Spiritual Gifts because they are manifested at different times and in different ways by *all* Spirit filled believers. And, regardless of the variations of these *gifts*, they are bestowed by the Holy Spirit, who is the same in every believer. This provides unity in the operation, acceptance and appreciation of Spiritual Gifts in the Body of Christ.

Typifying the human body, Paul teaches that God gives special attention to parts of the body that are weaker in comparison to other parts, so that the whole body would be strong and equal in appearance. This illustrates how useful all *gifts* are to the Body of Christ, none being more important than the other.

1ˢᵗ Corinthians 12:12-27 "For as the body is one, and hath many members, and all the members of that one body, being many, are one body: so also is Christ. For by one Spirit are we all baptized into one body, whether we be Jews or Gentiles, whether we be bond or free; and have been all made to drink into one Spirit. For the body is not one member, but many. If the foot shall say, Because I am not the hand, I am not of the body; is it therefore not of the body? And if the ear shall say, Because I am not the eye, I am not of the body; is it therefore not of the body? If the whole body were an eye, where were the hearing? If the whole were hearing, where were the smelling? But now hath God set the members every one of them in the body, as it hath pleased him. And if they were all one member, where were the body? But now are they many members, yet but one body. And the eye cannot say unto the hand, I have no need of thee: nor again the head to the feet, I have no need of you. Nay, much more those members of the body, which seem to be more feeble, are necessary: And those members of the body, which we think to be less honorable, upon these we bestow more abundant honour; and our uncomely parts have more abundant comeliness. For our comely parts have no need: but God hath tempered the body together, having given more abundant honour to that part which lacked: That there should be no schism in the body; but that the members should have the same care one for another. And whether one member suffer, all the members suffer with it; or one member be honoured, all the members rejoice with it. Now ye are the body of Christ, and members in particular."

NECESSITY OF ALL GIFTS

The combination of Ministry Gifts and Spiritual Gifts also prove that all *gifts* are necessary and are equally important to balance the Body of Christ.

1st Corinthians 12:28-31 "And God hath set some in the church, first apostles, secondarily prophets, thirdly teachers, after that miracles, then gifts of healings, helps, governments, diversities of tongues. Are all apostles? are all prophets? are all teachers? are all workers of miracles? Have all the gifts of healing? do all speak with tongues? do all interpret? But covet earnestly the best gifts: and yet shew I unto you a more excellent way."

Ephesians 4:11 "Now these are the gifts Christ gave to the church: the apostles, the prophets, the evangelists, and the pastors and teachers." New Living Translation

OPERATION OF THE GIFTS

Because God is not the author of confusion, the operation of Spiritual Gifts necessitates control and balance so that their purpose *(which is* to *edify the church)* may be accomplished. Although these gifts are spiritual and supernatural, members operating in these endowments should not reject the disciplines of self-control, and proving of the *gift* in operation by others for Divine authentication, if they are truly yielded to the Holy Spirit.

Although the Apostle Paul, teaches the regulation of speaking in tongues in the 14th Chapter of 1st Corinthians, his lesson is to be applied to all of the *gifts*.

NOTES

NOTES

SPIRITUAL GIFTS WORKSHEET

Which Spiritual Gifts to you have?

_____

_____

_____

_____

Describe how they are used.

_____

_____

_____

_____

_____

_____

_____

_____

_____

_____

_____

_____

_____

_____

_____

_____

_____

_____

CHAPTER FIVE

DESCRIPTION OF SPIRITUAL GIFTS

THE WORD OF WISDOM – is the ability to speak words that are filled with divine wisdom, interpret dreams and visions with insight and give sound warnings, directions and instructions.

1st Corinthians 2:8 "The wisdom which none of the rulers of this age has understood; for if they had understood it, they would not have crucified the Lord of glory."

THE WORD OF KNOWLEDGE – is having divine knowledge and understanding of the principals of Christian faith, doctrines, morality and the ability to discern the true movement of God.

Colossians 2:2-7 "That their hearts may be encouraged, having been knit together in love, and attaining to all the wealth that comes from the full assurance of understanding resulting in a true knowledge of God's mystery, that is Christ Himself, in whom are hidden all the treasures of wisdom and knowledge. I say this in order that no one may delude you with persuasive argument. For even though I am absent in body, nevertheless I am with you in spirit, rejoicing to see your good discipline and the stability of your faith in Christ. As you therefore have received Christ Jesus the Lord, so walk in Him, having been firmly rooted and now being built up in Him and established in your faith, just as you were instructed, and overflowing with gratitude."

THE GIFT OF FAITH – this type of faith differs from the faith that is involved with Salvation and our faith as Christians.

Romans 1:16 "For I am not ashamed of the gospel of Christ: for it is the power of God unto salvation to every on that believeth; to the Jew first, and also to the Greek."

James 2:14-20 "What doth it profit, my brethren, though a man say he hath faith, and have not works? Can faith save him? If a brother or sister e naked, and destitute of daily food, And one of you say unto them, Depart in peace, by ye warmed and filled; notwithstanding ye give them not those things which are needful to the body; what doth it profit? Even so faith, if it hath not works is dead, being alone."

Faith here is an *"endowment"* that is exhibited by having a super-natural ability to firmly trust God in the time of crisis.

Mark 11:22-24 "And Jesus answered saying to them, 'Have faith in God. Truly I say to you, whoever says to this mountain, be taken up and cast into the sea, and does not doubt in his heart, but believes that what he says is going to happen, it shall be granted him. Therefore I say to you, all things for which you pray and ask, believe that you have received them, and they shall be granted you." New American Standard Bible

THE GIFT OF HEALING – the ability to minister health *(give service, care* or *aid)* to someone else in a spiritual way.

Acts 28:7-9 "In the same quarters were possessions of the chief man of the island, whose name was Publius; who received us, and lodged us three days courteously. And it came to pass, that the father of Publius lay sick of a fever and of a bloody flux: to whom Paul entered in, and prayed, and laid his hands on him, and healed him. So when this was done, which had diseases in the island, came and were healed."

THE WORKING OF MIRACLES – God exuding His power through a believer who has strong faith.

Acts 19:11-12 "And God wrought special miracles by the hands of Paul: So that from his body were brought unto the sick handkerchiefs and aprons, and the diseases departed from them, and the evil spirits went out of them."

DISCERNING OF SPIRITS – gives us the spiritual ability to identify evil spirits that operate through others in order to safeguard our spirituality and faith.

1st John 4:1 "Beloved, believe not every spirit, but try the spirits whether they are of God: because many false prophets are gone out into the world."

THE GIFT OF PROPHECY – unlike the messages from the Prophets of the Old Testament, this *gift* is intended to edify, inform, and exhort the Body of Christ.

1ˢᵗ Corinthians 14:3 "But he that prophesieth speaking unto men to edification, and exhortation, and comfort."

DIVERSE TONGUES AND INTERPRETATION OF TONGUES – the supernatural language of tongues is a gift that is used to speak to God. This language *is:*

1. Different and unfamiliar
2. A person's prayer language when there is no interpretation
3. Interpreted only when God sends a message to be understood by everyone else
4. Cannot be understood by evil spirits
5. Should be used with discretion

1ˢᵗ Corinthians 14:14 "For if I pray in an unknown tongue, my spirit prayeth, but my understanding is unfruitful."

1ˢᵗ Corinthians 14:23 "If therefore the whole church be come together into one place and all speak with tongues, there come in those that are unlearned, or unbelievers, will they not say that we are mad?"

1ˢᵗ Corinthians 14:27 "If any man speak in an unknown tongue, let it be by two, or at the most by three, and that by course; and let one interpret. But if there be no interpreter, let him keep silence in the church; and let him speak *(pray in tongues)* to himself, and to God."

OTHER SPIRITUAL GIFTS

1ˢᵗ Corinthians 12:28 "And God hath set some in the church, first apostles, secondarily prophets, thirdly teachers, after that miracles, then gifts of healings, helps, governments, diversities of tongues." Read Romans 12:3-8 for more Spiritual Gifts

In this passage of Scripture there are two other *gifts* that are seldom identified as spiritual endowments; they are the *gifts* of helps and

50

governments (administration). These *gifts* operate within the church through members who are reliable, consistent and whom we consider to be talented. Although these individuals are not always recognized as being "Spiritual Gifts" to the Body of Christ, they play a vital role in the growth and stability of the church.

THE GIFT OF HELPS – is also referred to as the "Gift of Ministering." These are members of the Body of Christ who have the spiritual willingness to assist ministers in their leadership roles as well as members of the church. They give their time, resources and lend a hand whenever and however they can without looking to be rewarded.

THE GIFT OF GOVERNMENTS OR ADMINISTRATIONS – are the members of the church who lead and guide others without overstepping their boundaries or authority. They operate in the spirit of excellence using their talent and professional expertise for the best interest of the Body of Christ.

Various translations of 1st Corinthians 12:28

New International Version
"And God has placed in the church first of all apostles, second prophets, third teachers, then miracles, then gifts of healing, of helping, of guidance, and of different kinds of tongues."

New Living Translation
"Here are some of the parts God has appointed for the church: first are apostles, second are prophets, third are teachers, then those who do miracles, those who have the gift of healing, those who can help others, those who have the gift of leadership, those who speak in unknown languages."

English Standard Version
"And God has appointed in the church first apostles, second prophets, third teachers, then miracles, then gifts of healing, helping, administrating, and various kinds of tongues."

New American Standard Bible

"And God has appointed in the church, first apostles, second prophets, third teachers, then miracles, then gifts of healings, helps, administrations, various kinds of tongues."

International Standard Version

"God has appointed in the church first of all apostles, second prophets, third teachers, then those who perform miracles, those who have gifts of healing, those who help others, administrators, and those who speak various kinds of languages."

NOTES

NOTES

CHAPTER SIX

INTRODUCTION TO MINISTRY GIFTS

Definition: *"Gift"* is from the Greek translation *"endowment."* This means that the Lord, endows specific individuals with all that is necessary to operate in a ministry office. These individuals may show signs of being a "Ministry Gift" to the Body of Christ without much effort because of the Divine nature of their endowment. Because ministry offices are gifts to the Body of Christ, we cannot self-appoint ourselves into an office.

MINISTRY GIFTS

The Ministry Gifts to the Body of Christ outlined in the Scriptures are the Apostles, Prophets, Evangelists, Pastors, Teachers.

1st Corinthians 12:28 "And in the church God has appointed first of all apostles, second prophets, third teachers, then workers of miracles, and those with gifts of healing, helping, administration, and various tongues."

Ephesians 4:11-12 "And he gave some, apostles; and some, prophets; and some, evangelists; and some, pastors and teachers. For the perfecting of the saints, for the work of the ministry, for the edifying of the body of Christ:"

THE CHURCH

Definition: *"Church"* is from the Greek meaning "Called Out." The Church is where the mission of God is carried out under the headship and authority of Jesus Christ with the empowerment of the Holy Spirit. It is also referred to as "The Congregation" *(consisting of any number of people),* "A group of Christians in one location," "The Saints," *(All Believers in Christ on earth)* and "The Body of Christ."

Matthew 18:20 "For where two or three are gathered together in my name, there am I in the midst of them."

Acts 20:28 "Take heed therefore unto yourselves, and to all the flock, over the which the Holy Ghost hath made you overseers, to feed the church of God, which he hath purchased with his own blood."

Revelation 14:12 "Here is the patience of the saints: here [are] they that keep the commandments of God, and the faith of Jesus."

Ephesians 1:22-23 "And hath put all *things* under his feet, and gave him *to be* the head over all *things* to the church, Which is his body, the fulness of him that filleth all in all."

Christ, being the head of the Church has the authority to appoint specific individuals as "Ministry Gifts" to the Church and will award them for their service.

Philippians 2:9-11 "Wherefore God also hath highly exalted him, and given him a name which is above every name: That at the name of Jesus every knee should bow, of *things* in heaven, and *things* in earth, and *things* under the earth; And *that* every tongue should confess that Jesus Christ *is* Lord, to the glory of God the Father."

Ephesians 4:11 "And he gave some, apostles; and some, prophets; and some, evangelists; and some, pastors and teachers."

Revelation 22:12 "And, behold, I come quickly; and my reward is with me, to give every man according as his work shall be."

THE REASONS FOR THE MINISTRY GIFTS

Ministry Gifts are given to the Body of Christ to help its members grow and mature. The word *"edify"* means to build-up, instruct and uplift.

Ephesians 4:12 "For the perfecting of the saints, for the work of the ministry, for the edifying of the body of Christ."

The function of a "Ministry Gift" differs from that of a "Spiritual Gift." A person endowed to be a "Ministry Gift" is placed in a ministerial office with supernatural abilities to perform within that office on a continual basis. "Spiritual Gifts" operate upon Church members as the Holy Spirit wills.

1st Corinthians 12:10 "To another the working of miracles; to

another prophecy; to another discerning of spirits; to another *divers* kinds of tongues; to another the interpretation of tongues."

1ˢᵗ Corinthians 12:28 "And God hath set some in the church, first apostles, secondarily prophets, thirdly teachers, after that miracles, then gifts of healings, helps, governments, diversities of tongues."

THE INVOLVEMENT OF THE GODHEAD

GOD THE FATHER

1ˢᵗ Corinthians 12:27-28 "Now ye are the body of Christ, and members in particular. And God hath set some in the church, first apostles, secondarily prophets, thirdly teachers, after that miracles, then gifts of healings, helps, governments, diversities of tongues."

JESUS CHRIST

Ephesians 4:7-8 "But unto every one of us is given grace according to the measure of the gift of Christ. Wherefore he saith, when he ascended up on high, he led captivity captive, and gave gifts unto men."

THE HOLY SPIRIT

1ˢᵗ Corinthians 12:7 "Now to each one the manifestation of the Spirit is given for the common good."

NOTES

NOTES

CHAPTER SEVEN

DESCRIPTION OF MINISTRY GIFTS

THE APOSTLE

IS SENT

Mark 3:13-14 "Afterward Jesus went up on a mountain and called out the ones he wanted to go with him. And they came to him. Then he appointed twelve of them and called them his apostles. They were to accompany him, and he would send them out to preach," New American Standard

ESTABLISHES MINISTRIES, HAS EXCEPTIONAL ORGANIZATIONAL SKILLS, LEADS AND INSTRUCTS GOD'S PEOPLE with spiritual proficiency.

1ˢᵗ Corinthians 3:10 "According to the grace of God which is given unto me, as a wise masterbuilder, I have laid the foundation, and another buildeth thereon. But let every man take heed how he buildeth thereupon."

HAS SPECIAL AUTHORITY TO GOVERN CHURCHES

Because Apostles are spiritually equipped to launch churches, they also govern and have ministerial authority over them.

2ⁿᵈ Corinthians 10:8-9 "For though I should boast somewhat more of our authority, which the Lord hath given us for edification, and not for your destruction, I should not be ashamed: That I may not seem as if I would terrify you by letters."

WORKS SIGNS AND WONDERS – that confirms their preaching, work and ministry office.

Mark 16:19-20 "So then after the Lord had spoken unto them, he was received up into heaven, and sat on the right hand of God. And they went forth, and preached everywhere, the Lord working with them, and confirming the word with signs following. Amen."

2ⁿᵈ Corinthians 12:12 "I persevered in demonstrating among you the marks of a true apostle, including signs, wonders and miracles."

Acts 19:11 "God gave Paul the power to perform unusual miracles." New Living Translation

THE APOSTLES OF CHRIST

The Apostles of Christ also called the "Twelve Apostles of the Lamb" were ordained as such because they witnessed His death, resurrection and ascension.

Luke 24:48 "And ye are witnesses of these things."

Acts 1:9 "And when he had spoken these things, while they beheld, he was taken up; and a cloud received him out of their sight."

The answer to the question of the Ministry Office of the Apostle being fulfilled in present times is *"yes"* based on these *facts:*

a) Apostles are *"gifts"* to the Body of Christ for the purpose of *"equipping"* its members for service and spiritual growth.

   Ephesians 4:12 "For the equipping of the saints for the work of service, to the building up of the body of Christ."

   Ephesians 5:27 "That He might present to Himself the church in all her glory, having no spot or wrinkle or any such thing; but that she should be holy and blameless."

b) Being a Divine *"gift"* the office of the Apostle is not taken back by God.

   Romans 11:29 "For God's gifts and his call can never be withdrawn." New Living Translation

c) From the call of Paul, we learn that others can have a close supernatural encounter with Christ to be set apart in the office by Him. This proves that there are Apostles besides the twelve Apostles of the Lamb.

   Act 9:3 "And as he journeyed, he came near Damascus: and

suddenly there shined round about him a light from heaven."

1st Corinthians 9:1 "Am I not free? Am I not an apostle? Have I not seen Jesus our Lord? Are you not the result of my work in the Lord?" New International Version

The Apostle Paul is considered as one of the greatest Apostles to the Church. However, the greatest of all Apostles is Jesus Christ.

Hebrews 3:1 "Therefore, holy brethren, partakers of a heavenly calling, consider Jesus, the Apostle and High Priest of our confession."

THE PROPHET

Unlike Old Testament prophets who preached God's Will, warned against sin, gave instructions, revealed impending judgements and foretold future events, the "Ministry Gift" of a Prophet is different because *they are:*

- Ministers that serve others
- Teachers with spiritual insight into the Scriptures to interpret their deep truths
- Preachers and proclaimers of the Gospel of Jesus Christ
- Revelators that also utilize the Spiritual Gifts of The Word of Wisdom, The Word of Knowledge and Discerning of Spirits
- Anointed to give "personal prophecies" more than national or corporate foretelling.

Acts 21:10-11 "And as we tarried *there* many days, there came down from Judaea a certain prophet, named Agabus. And when he was come unto us, he took Paul's girdle, and bound his own hands and feet, and said, Thus saith the Holy Ghost, So shall the Jews at Jerusalem bind the man that owneth this girdle, and shall deliver *him* into the hands of the Gentiles."

Acts 11:28 "And there stood up one of them named Agabus,

and signified by the spirit that there should be great dearth throughout all the world: which came to pass in the days of Claudius Caesar."

ERRORS CONCERNING THE OFFICE OF THE PROPHET

1. Paying for a prophetic Word from God: A Prophet is a minister and as such should not use their endowment for monetary gain.

2. Continuously seeking a Word of Prophecy: Relying on Prophets for their supernatural revelations and prophecies will hinder the Holy Spirit from giving us the discernment and insight that we personally need. Jesus dealt very harshly with the multitudes that sought Him for confirmations and signs; which proves that He does not approve of this behavior.

3. Expecting more than what was given: We should remember that prophets speak what they Divinely receive. Anything other than that will be from a human source. Prompting a prophet to be specific with dates, times, seasons or details that are not part of the prophetic message will give false expectations.

CONFUSING THE MINISTRY OFFICE OF THE PROPHET

We must be careful not to confuse the office of the Prophet with the "Spiritual Gift of Prophecy." The distinction between the two is:

The Spiritual Gift of Prophecy can be exercised by any member of the Body of Christ at any given time

The Ministry Gift of a Prophet to the Body of Christ" is a minister who fulfills all of the ministerial duties of that office with supernatural characteristics and abilities on a continual basis

THE EVANGELIST

A careful study of the Eighth Chapter of the Book of Acts teaches us that an *Evangelist:*

TRAVELS FROM PLACE TO PLACE PREACHING THE GOSPEL

Acts 8:25 "And they, when they had testified and preached the word of the Lord, returned to Jerusalem, and preached the gospel in many villages of the Samaritans."

Acts 8:40 "But Philip was found at Azotus: and passing through he preached in all the cities, till he came to Caesarea."

IS DIVINELY APPOINTED to specific locations to fulfill special ministry needs.

Acts 8:26 "And the angel of the Lord spake unto Philip, saying, Arise, and go toward the south unto the way that goeth down from Jerusalem unto Gaza, which is desert."

WORKS MIRACLES

Acts 8:4-8 "Therefore they that were scattered abroad went everywhere preaching the word. Then Philip went down to the city of Samaria, and preached Christ unto them. And the people with one accord gave heed unto those things which Philip spake, hearing and seeing the miracles which he did. For unclean spirits, crying with loud voice, came out of many that were possessed with them: and many taken with palsies, and that were lame, were healed. And there was great joy in that city."

IS PREPARED AT ALL TIMES WITH THE WORD OF GOD

2ⁿᵈ Timothy 4:2 "Preach the word of God. Be prepared, whether the time is favorable or not. Patiently correct, rebuke *(reprimand, admonish)*, and encourage your people with good teaching." New Living Translation

IS A SOUL WINNER – which is the main priority of the Evangelist.

Acts 8:12 "But when they believed Philip preaching the things concerning the kingdom of God, and the name of Jesus Christ, they were baptized, both men and women."

PREACHES JESUS – which is the core of their evangelical message.

Acts 8:5 "Then Philip went down to the city of Samaria, and preached Christ unto them."

ENDURES HARDSHIP – this is mainly because of their evangelical preaching that targets behavior and sin. This makes the Evangelist less welcomed, yet at the same time very appreciated.

2nd Timothy 4:3-5 "For the time will come when people will not put up with sound doctrine. Instead, to suit their own desires, they will gather around them a great number of teachers to say what their itching ears want to hear. They will turn their ears away from the truth and turn aside to myths. But you, keep your head in all situations, endure hardship, do the work of an evangelist, discharge all the duties of your ministry." New International Version

ALWAYS MEETS THE NEEDS OF THE PEOPLE through their evangelistic message because *they:*

1. Have a close relationship with the Lord

2. Are Divinely inspired

3. Do not let hardship limited their commitment and purpose

Acts 8:30-31 "And Philip ran thither to *him*, and heard him read the prophet Esaias, and said, Understandest thou what thou readest? And he said, How can I, except some man should guide me? And he desired Philip that he would come up and sit with him."

THE PASTOR

Definition: *"Pastor"* is from the Greek meaning Shepherd. Other names for a Pastor *are:*

OVERSEER AND BISHOP – usually over a number of churches.

Acts 20:28 "Take heed therefore unto yourselves, and to all the flock, over which the Holy Ghost hath made you overseers, to feed the church of God, which he hath purchased with his own blood."

1ˢᵗ Timothy 3:1 "This *is* a true saying, If a man desire the office of a bishop, he desireth a good work."

THE FUNCTIONS OF A PASTOR *are to:*

LEAD AND GUIDE

Psalm 23:1-3 (A Psalm of David) "The LORD is my shepherd; I shall not want. He maketh me to lie down in green pastures: he leadeth me beside the still waters. He restoreth my soul: he leadeth me in the paths of righteousness for his name's sake."

PROVIDE CARE

Isaiah 40:11 "He shall feed his flock like a shepherd: he shall gather the lambs with his arm, and carry *them* in his bosom, *and* shall gently lead those that are with young."

DEFEND AND PROTECT

John 10:11-14 "I am the good shepherd: the good shepherd giveth his life for the sheep. But he that is an hireling, and not the shepherd, whose own the sheep are not, seeth the wolf coming, and leaveth the sheep, and fleeth: and the wolf catcheth them, and scattereth the sheep. The hireling fleeth, because he is an hireling, and careth not for the sheep. I am the good shepherd, and know my *sheep*, and am known of mine."

TEACH

Jeremiah 3:15 "And I will give you shepherds after my own heart, who will feed you with knowledge and understanding."
English Standard Version

REQUIREMENTS FOR THE OFFICE OF THE PASTOR

1ˢᵗ Timothy 3:1-6 "It is a trustworthy statement: if any man aspires to the office of overseer, it is a fine work he desires *to do.* An overseer, then, must be above reproach, the husband of one wife, temperate, prudent, respectable, hospitable, able to teach, not addicted to wine or pugnacious, but gentle, peaceable, free from the love of money. *He must be* one who manages his own household well, keeping his children under control with all dignity (but if a man does not know how to manage his own household, how will he take care of the church of God?), *and* not a new convert, so that he will not become conceited and fall into the condemnation incurred by the devil. And he must have a good reputation with those outside *the church,* so that he will not fall into reproach and the snare of the devil." New American Standard Bible

According to this passage of Scripture, a Pastor *must be:*

- above reproach (*criticism, blame)*
- the husband of one wife
- temperate *(calm)*
- prudent *(wise, sensible)*
- respectable
- hospitable
- able to teach
- not addicted to wine or pugnacious *(confrontational, belligerent)*
- gentle
- peaceable
- free from the love of money

And must be:

- one who manages his own household well, keeping his children under control with dignity
- experienced, so that they will not become conceited
- have a good reputation with those outside of the church, so that they will not fall into reproach and the snare of the devil

Finally, a Pastor must have a Shepherd's Heart.

John 21:15 "So when they had dined, Jesus saith to Simon Peter, Simon, *son* of Jonas, lovest thou me more than these? He saith unto him, Yea, Lord; thou knowest that I love thee. He saith unto him, Feed my lambs."

Jesus fulfilled the "Ministry Office" of the Pastor as "The Great Shepherd," "The Chief Shepherd" and "The Good Shepherd."

Hebrews 13:20 "Now the God of peace, that brought again from the dead our Lord Jesus, that great shepherd of the sheep, through the blood of the everlasting covenant."

1st Peter 2:25 "For ye were as sheep going astray; but are now returned unto the Shepherd and Bishop of your souls."

John 10:14 "I am the good shepherd, and know my *sheep*, and am known of mine."

Read 2nd Timothy, Chapters 3, 4, 5 and Titus, Chapter 2 to learn more on the qualifications and responsibilities of the Pastoral Office.

THE TEACHER

Timothy, a newly assigned Pastor is instructed by The Apostle Paul, to include teaching of the Word of God in his ministry. This shows a combination of the Ministry Gifts of the Pastor and the Teacher.

1st Timothy 4:11 "These things command and teach."

Characteristically, *Teachers:*

- Give instructions with sound doctrine
- Have Divine insight into the Scriptures which makes their ministry somewhat prophetic
- Are spiritually inspired, insightful and motivated regarding the Word of God, which distinguishes them from secular teachers

1st Corinthians 2:12-13 "Now we have received, not the spirit of the world, but the spirit which is of God; that we might know the things that are freely given to us of God. Which things also we speak, not in the words which man's wisdom teacheth, but which the Holy Ghost teacheth; comparing spiritual things with spiritual."

1ˢᵗ Timothy 4:16 "Take heed unto thyself, and unto the doctrine; continue in them: for in doing this thou shalt both save thyself, and them that hear thee."

FACTS TO REMEMBER REGARDING MINISTRY GIFTS:

1. One cannot place them self in the Body of Christ as a "Ministry Gift"

2. The Listing of "Ministry Gifts" do not depict their order of importance to the Church

3. Each "Ministry Gift" has Divine peculiarities associated with them

4. Ministry Gifts are not to be used in corruptible ways

5. Although their qualifications are practically the same, Elders are not to be confused with fulfilling the office of a Pastor. They are appointed to oversee the general functions of the church because of their age and experience.

Titus 1:5-9 "For this cause left I thee in Crete, that thou shouldest set in order the things that are wanting, and ordain elders in every city, as I had appointed thee: If any be blameless, the husband of one wife, having faithful children not accused of riot or unruly. For a bishop must be blameless, as the steward of God; not selfwilled, not soon angry, not given to wine, no striker, not given to filthy lucre; But a lover of hospitality, a lover of good men, sober, just, holy, temperate; Holding fast the faithful word as he hath been taught, that he may be able by sound doctrine both to exhort and to convince the gainsayers."

NOTES

NOTES

MINISTRY GIFTS WORKSHEET

Do you feel that you are called to a Ministry Office?

_____

_____

_____

_____

If yes, which one?

_____

_____

_____

Describe how you operate in that office.

_____

_____

_____

_____

_____

_____

_____

_____

_____

_____

_____

_____

_____

_____

1ˢᵗ Corinthians 12:28 "And God hath set some in the church, first apostles, secondarily prophets, thirdly teachers, after that miracles, <u>then</u> gifts of healings, helps, governments, diversities of tongues.

What are the two categories of "Gifts" in this Scripture?

1. _____

2. _____

Explain the above Scripture putting emphasis on the underlined word.

_____
_____
_____
_____
_____
_____
_____
_____
_____
_____
_____
_____
_____
_____
_____
_____
_____
_____
_____

Explain why you cannot appoint yourself as a "Ministry Gift" to the Body of Christ.

_____

_____

_____

_____

_____

_____

_____

_____

_____

_____

_____

_____

_____

_____

_____

_____

_____

_____

_____

_____

_____

_____

CHAPTER EIGHT

PRACTICAL EVANGELISM

An Evangelist is a person who preaches the Gospel, traveling from place to place. In essence, they are a messenger of the Good News. The only specific New Testament references to the work of an Evangelist are found in Acts 21:8, 2nd Timothy 4:5 and Ephesians 4:11.

Acts 21:8 "And on the next day we departed and came to Caesarea; and entering the house of Philip the evangelist, who was one of the seven, we stayed with him."

2nd Timothy 4:5 "But you, be sober in all things, endure hardship, do the work of an evangelist, fulfill your ministry."

Ephesians 4:11 "And He gave some as apostles, and some as prophets, and some as evangelists, and some as pastors and teachers."

CHARACTERISTICS OF AN EVANGELIST

Two of the most noticeable characteristics of an Evangelist *are:*

- Their Message is always centered around Christ's Deity, ministry and purpose
- The Supernatural operation of the gifts of healing and working of miracles *(signs)* confirm the ministry of the Evangelist

Acts 8:5-8 "And Philip went down to the city of Samaria and began proclaiming Christ to them. And the multitudes with one accord were giving attention to what was said by Philip, as they heard and saw the signs which he was performing. For in the case of many who had unclean spirits, they were coming out of them shouting with a loud voice; and many who had been paralyzed and lame were healed. And there was much rejoicing in that city."

From this we learn that the Evangelist is endowed with spiritual gifts that are necessary to fulfill their office. They will operate in their calling with Divine power that will draw people to their ministry. And, their anointing to preach God's Word will heal, deliver and save souls.

Utilizing their charisma *(gift)*, the Evangelist must remain humble and realize that the anointing, signs and wonders that are associated with their ministry is by God's Power and not their own.

THE MESSAGE OF THE EVANGELIST

The Evangelist will demonstrate the following attributes in their message; it *will:*

BE INSPIRED – by God and is highly anointed so that it breaks yokes.

Isaiah 10:27 "And it shall come to pass in that day, that his burden shall be taken away from off thy shoulder, and his yoke from off thy neck, and the yoke shall be destroyed because of the anointing."

FOCUS ON CHRIST

The focal point of every Evangelistic message is Christ. For example while in Samaria, Philip only preached about Jesus Christ. The people who thought too highly of Simon, were convicted of their error when they heard Philip's message.

Acts 8:5 "And Philip went down to the city of Samaria and began proclaiming Christ to them."

MEET THE IMMEDIATE NEEDS OF THE PEOPLE HEARING IT

The evangelistic message will definitely correspond with the immediate needs of the people hearing it. This is also exemplified by Philip's ministry to the Ethiopian eunuch in Acts 8:26-36. The Ethiopian is described as a "Godly man," who was reading the book of Isaiah while returning from the temple in Jerusalem. Philip, being sent by the Lord, explained what he was reading to him. This was exactly what he needed to be converted and baptized.

Acts 8:26-36 "As for Philip, an angel of the Lord said to him, "Go south down the desert road that runs from Jerusalem to Gaza.""

So he started out, and he met the treasurer of Ethiopia, a eunuch of great authority under the Kandake, the queen of Ethiopia. The eunuch had gone to Jerusalem to worship, and he was now returning. Seated in his carriage, he was reading aloud from the book of the prophet Isaiah. The Holy Spirit said to Philip, "Go over and walk along beside the carriage." Philip ran over and heard the man reading from the prophet Isaiah. Philip asked, "Do you understand what you are reading?" The man replied, "How can I, unless someone instructs me?" And he urged Philip to come up into the carriage and sit with him. The passage of Scripture he had been reading was this: "He was led like a sheep to the slaughter. And as a lamb is silent before the shearers, he did not open his mouth. He was humiliated and received no justice. Who can speak of his descendants? For his life was taken from the earth." The eunuch asked Philip, "Tell me, was the prophet talking about himself or someone else?" So beginning with this same Scripture, Philip told him the Good News about Jesus. As they rode along, they came to some water, and the eunuch said, "Look! There's some water! Why can't I be baptized?" He ordered the carriage to stop, and they went down into the water, and Philip baptized him." American Standard Version

THE EVANGELIST IS GOD'S MESSENGER

Through the ministry of the Evangelist, God reveals His Divine Will. The Evangelist therefore *must:*

- Live a holy and consecrated life which includes fasting and much prayer

- Study and meditate on God's Word

- Exercise wisdom and discernment while ministering, especially because they are God's spokesperson who will reveal the truth

- Minister in love to correspond with God's nature concerning souls

Taking all these facts into careful consideration, there are messages from God that are considered timely for the saved, unsaved as well as the entire Body of Christ...the Church. It is therefore, not uncommon that an Evangelist will preach for a while on a specific subject. Common and more frequent subjects *are:*

SIN

Romans 3:23 "For all have sinned and fall short of the glory of God."

THE CONSEQUENCES OF SIN

Romans 6:23 "For the wages of sin is death, but the free gift of God is eternal life in Christ Jesus our Lord."

ETERNAL LIFE AND DEATH

Revelation 20:15 "And if anyone's name was not found written in the book of life, he was thrown into the lake of fire."

GOD'S REMEDY FOR SIN

John 3:16 "For God so loved the world, that He gave His only begotten son, that whoever believes in Him should not perish, but have eternal life."

THE WORK OF CHRIST

Isaiah 53:5-6 "But He was pierced through for our transgressions, He was crushed of our iniquities; The chastening for our well-being fell upon Him, And by His scourging we are healed. All of us like sheep have gone astray, Each of us has turned to his own way; But the LORD has caused the iniquity of us all to fall on Him."

THE AUTHORITY OF GOD'S WORD

2nd Timothy 3:16 "All Scripture is inspired by God and profitable for teaching, for reproof, for correction, for training in righteousness."

NEW LIFE IN CHRIST

2nd Corinthians 5:17 "Therefore if any man is in Christ, he is a new creature; the old things passed away; behold, new things have come."

THE HOLY SPIRIT

Romans 8:1-4 "There is therefore now no condemnation for those who are in Christ Jesus.' For the law of the Spirit of life in Christ Jesus has set you free from the law of sin and of death. For what the Law could not do, weak as it was through the flesh, God did: sending His own Son in the likeness of sinful flesh and as an offering for sin, He condemned sin in the flesh, in order that the requirement of the Law might be fulfilled in us who do not walk according to the flesh, but according to the Spirit."

LIVING A LIFE OF VICTORY

Philippians 4:13 "I can do all things through Him who strengthens me."

RENEWED HOPE

Titus 2:13 "Looking for the blessed hope and the appearing of the glory of our great God and Savior, Christ Jesus."

1st Thessalonians 4:16-17 "For the Lord Himself will descend from heaven with a shout, with the voice of the archangel, and with the trumpet of God; and the dead in Christ shall rise first. Then we who are alive and remain shall be caught up together with them in the clouds to meet the Lord in the air, and thus we shall always be with the Lord."

THE EVANGELIST IS A SOUL WINNER

The Evangelist has a burden for lost souls and seeks to bring them to Christ *(i.e. a soul winner)*. This requires them to have patience and knowledge to address opposition to their message. Lost souls are among many classes of people with different opinions on salvation and the way they live their lives. Here are a *few:*

"YOU ONLY HAVE ONE LIFE, SO LIVE IT FOR TODAY!"

Life after death is a non-reality to many people. Because of the lack of sound Bible Doctrine and Biblical truth, these individuals strongly believe that living life for the present is most important because after that "who knows?"

Response: A suitable response to this person is the reality of life after death. They would need to understand the penalty for rejecting the Son of God, and the judgment associated with it.

Hebrews 9:27 "And inasmuch as it is appointed for men to die once and after this comes judgment."

Revelation 20:11-15 "And I saw a great white throne and Him who sat upon it, from whose presence earth and heaven fled away, and no place was found for them. And I saw the dead, the great and the small, standing before the throne, and books were opened; and another book was opened, which is the book of life; and the dead were judged from the things which were written in the books, according to their deeds. And the sea gave up the dead which were in it, and death and Hades gave up the dead which were in them; and they were judged, everyone of them according to their deeds. And death and Hades were thrown into the lake of fire. This is the second death, the lake of fire. And if anyone's name was not found written in the book of life, he was thrown into the lake of fire."

"I HAVE TOO MUCH TO GIVE UP"

Many people feel that the Bible dictates far too many complicated examples of righteousness. They view the Bible as a book of restrictions and overwhelming sacrifices. Evaluating their lifestyles, accomplishments and possessions, they feel that there would be too much to lose or give up to live a Christian lifestyle.

Response: These people should be told the story of the rich man and Lazarus. Further, they should be patiently taught that our natural minds cannot understand the things of God because those things are spiritual. And because of that, we would have to think about them with a spiritual mind-set *(spiritually discerned)*. Thus, the solution to understanding the Bible is to accept Christ as their Lord and Savior and be born again.

Luke 16:22-25 "Now it came about that the poor man died and he was carried away by the angels to Abraham's bosom; and the rich man also died and was buried. And in Hades he lifted up his eyes, being in torment, and saw Abraham far away, and Lazarus in his bosom. And he cried out and said Father Abraham, have mercy on me, and send Lazarus, that he may dip the tip of his finger in water and cool off my tongue; for I am in agony in this flame. But Abraham said, 'Child, remember that during your life you received your good things, and likewise Lazarus bad things; but now he is being comforted here, and you are in agony.'"

1ˢᵗ Corinthians 2:14 "But a natural man does not accept the things of the Spirit of God; for they are foolishness to him, and he cannot understand them, because they are spiritually appraised."

"I'M A GOOD PERSON"

There are those who believe that being a good person is all that is necessary to please God. The real pity in these cases is that they are clinging to a "false hope."

Response: The self-righteous must clearly understand that there is no Salvation in simply being a good person. The only way to be saved is by the propitiatory *(the part of Christ's sacrifice that made peace between us and God, giving us favor with Him)* work of Jesus Christ.

Romans 3:10 "As it is written, 'There is none righteous, not even one.'"

Romans 3:24-26 "Being justified as a gift by His grace through the redemption which is in Christ Jesus; whom God displayed publicly as a propitiation in His blood through faith. This was to demonstrate His righteousness, because in the forbearance of God He passed over the sins previously committed; for the demonstration, I say of His righteousness at the present time, that He might be just and the justifier of the one who has faith in Jesus."

THE GOODNESS OF GOD

Then there are the people who only focus on God's attributes of love, mercy and goodness. They overlook His other attributes of holiness, righteousness and ensuing judgement for sin.

Response: A clear explanation of God's expectations for holiness and righteous living is necessary. They would need to know that there is definitely punishment for sin, ungodly living, deliberate defiance to God's standards for mankind and rejection of Christ who was sent to deliver them.

Genesis 18:25 "Far be it from Thee to do such a thing, to slay the righteous with the wicked, so that the righteous and the wicked are treated alike. Far be it from Thee! Shall not the Judge of all the earth deal justly?"

Revelation 20:12 "And I saw the dead, the great and the small, standing before the throne, and books were opened; and another book was opened, which is the book of life; and the dead were judged from the things which were written in the books according to their deeds."

PREPARATION FOR SALVATION

Others feel that they have to prepare for salvation. They feel that putting their lives in order is solely their responsibility. Guilt, condemnation and fear of not being able to commit to a life of godliness, are the main reasons for their struggle.

Response: Guidance and a sympathetic approach is most suitable in these cases. With patience and care, they will learn that all the forgiveness, strength and power is in Jesus Christ, the Savior of mankind. Eventually, they will give up and surrender their troubled lives to Jesus Christ.

1st Peter 5:7 "Casting all your anxiety upon Him, because

He cares for you."

Romans 8:1 "There is therefore now no condemnation for those who are in Christ Jesus"

NOTES

NOTES

CHAPTER NINE

PERSONAL EVANGELISM

Christ has commissioned every believer to win souls to Him through personal evangelism ... this is The Great Commission.

Mark 16:15 "And he said unto them, Go ye into all the world, and preach the gospel to every creature."

The Great Commission has two very effective methods for its fulfillment: *proclamation* and *affirmation*.

1. Proclamation has a prerequisite for its effectiveness and that is – we must have accepted Christ as our personal Lord and Savior before we can make announcements to other people about Salvation.

2. Affirmation to the Christian message is made *by:*

    *   How we live our life as a Christian *(which is more noticeable to others than we think)*

    *   What we say and how much we understand God's Word *(it is important to be careful of what we say or try to explain to others)*

    *   The Body of Christ – our church makes a big impression on people *(what it says and does can draw souls or turn them away)* Read James 2:1-9

THE MESSAGE WE GIVE

Knowledge is the foundation for effective soul winning. Therefore, we must have a thorough understanding of the Scriptures and Biblical facts.

In conjunction with this, is an awareness of what we are saying when we attempt to win a soul to Christ. Is our message centered on Christ? Are we placing more emphasis on specific parts of the Gospel of Salvation? Do we push as hard as we do because we want the achievement more than anything else?

Here are examples of the negative presentations that take away the potency of the Gospel of Christ and hinders true *soul winning:*

PREFERENCE DOCTRINES – is when we stress a particular doctrine over another because it was effective in our decision to accept Christ. We must remember that the other components in the in the process of Salvation are all equally important. For example if we highlight propitiation *(appease, make peace)* over grace *(favor)*, we have limited our witnessing to propitiation only. Complete Worksheet on Page 96.

THE BEST CHURCH – going to church is not the answer in and of itself when witnessing. Are we advertising our church because it *(in our opinion)* is the perfect church? We should not; because every church has its problems. This is natural because the church is an organism that is made up of many people who are not perfect.

The Gospel should not be minimized to going to "my church." The first focus should be on winning the soul to Christ. The place of fellowship, denomination, frequency of attendance, etc., should be suggested and explored with your help. In time, the person will find the place they feel the Lord has placed them.

RECEIVE IT NOW – is the pressure placed on someone to accept our message immediately, which could imply the motive of self-gratification. Wanting to fulfill the task of winning a soul is good, however, we should have the person's need of a Savior as the main priority, not achieving a goal.

We should always take into consideration that we may not be the only person to have witnessed to an individual. Could it be that we are the second whom the Lord has sent to water the seed of the Gospel that was placed in their heart by another? If so, then we have done our part and should celebrate how the Holy Spirit will bring that seed to full development to complete our task of winning a soul to Christ.

1st Corinthians 3:4-8 "When one of you says, "I am a follower of Paul," and another says, "I follow Apollos," aren't you acting just like people of the world? After all, who is Apollos? Who is

Paul? We are only God's servants through whom you believed the Good News. Each of us did the work the Lord gave us. I planted the seed in your hearts, and Apollos watered it, but it was God who made it grow. It's not important who does the planting, or who does the watering. What's important is that God makes the seed grow. The one who plants and the one who waters work together with the same purpose. And both will be rewarded for their own hard work." New Living Translation

The substance of our evangelism is to identify Jesus and His suffering for the redemption of mankind with no strings attached. We should realize this and not impose human standards, honor or tradition upon people when we witness.

NOTES

NOTES

PERSONAL EVANGELISM WORKSHEET

Which of the "Messages We Give" describes your emphasis when you witness?

_____

_____

_____

_____

Explain what you have learned about that type of witnessing and what you will do to correct it.

_____

_____

_____

_____

_____

_____

_____

_____

_____

_____

_____

_____

_____

_____

_____

_____

_____

_____

Define each of the following components that are included in the process of Salvation. Then, identify the one that helped you to give your life to Christ. Refer to page 91 "Preference Doctrines"

1. GRACE

_____

_____

_____

2. ATONEMENT

_____

_____

_____

3. SUBSTITUTION

_____

_____

_____

4. JUSTIFICATION

_____

_____

_____

5. SANCTIFICATION

_____

_____

_____

_____

CHAPTER TEN

REVIVAL SERVICES

Revival Services are held mainly to renew the spiritual life of believers. The excitement surrounding a Revival Service is the expectation that the Holy Spirit will move in a dynamic way to refill, refresh and empower church members. The overflow of a spirit-filled revival and the supernatural move of God, will also save the unsaved.

Acts 2:1- 4 "And when the day of Pentecost was fully come, they were all with one accord in one place. And suddenly there came a sound from heaven as of a rushing mighty wind, and it filled all the house where they were sitting. And there appeared unto them cloven tongues like as of fire, and it sat upon each of them. And they were all filled with the Holy Ghost, and began to speak with other tongues, as the Spirit gave them utterance."

Acts 4:23-31 "And being let go, they went to their own company, and reported all that the chief priests and elders had said unto them. And when they heard that, they lifted up their voice to God with one accord, and said, Lord, thou *art* God, which hast made heaven, and earth, and the sea, and all that in them is: Who by the mouth of thy servant David hast said, Why did the heathen rage, and the people imagine vain things? The kings of the earth stood up, and the rulers were gathered together against the Lord, and against his Christ. For of a truth against thy holy child Jesus, whom thou hast anointed, both Herod, and Pontius Pilate, with the Gentiles, and the people of Israel, were gathered together, For to do whatsoever thy hand and thy counsel determined before to be done. And now, Lord, behold their threatenings: and grant unto thy servants, that with all boldness they may speak thy word, By stretching forth thine hand to heal; and that signs and wonders may be done by the name of thy holy child Jesus. And when they had prayed, the place was shaken where they were assembled together; and they were all filled with the Holy Ghost, and they spake the word of God with boldness."

ORGANIZATION OF A REVIVAL SERVICE

Organization plays a very important role in having a successful Revival Service. Although Revival Services are attended mostly by believers, there will be a number of unbelievers, back sliders and people who have life issues in attendance. They should not come to the service to find confusion where they are seeking help and deliverance. We should also keep in mind that a lack of organization will hinder the move of God.

1st Corinthians 14:33 "For God is not a God of confusion but of peace, as in all the churches of the saints."

1st Corinthians 14:40 "But let all things be done properly and in an orderly manner."

An Evangelist should always remember that they are a "Ministry Gift" to the Body of Christ. Therefore, the Evangelist is a leader who has the responsibility *to:*

- Organize and oversee the Rival Service
- Train and meet with the members of the evangelist team
- Live a prayerful life
- Utilize the Spiritual Gift of Discernment
- Meet with the members of their evangelist team regularly

Keeping all of this in mind, we can agree that an organized evangelistic service is not left up to spontaneous decision making. Spontaneity in a highly anointed setting must be of Divine origin.

For Example: Worship and Praise leaders should not be left to minister on their own spontaneously. Rather, they *should:*

1. Meet with the Evangelist to discuss the music for the service
2. Attend all organizational meetings
3. Be part of special prayer for the Revival Service

Their responsibility is to lead the people in attendance into a joyful and spiritual worship experience. To do this requires skilled talent and knowledge that is infused with the anointing of God. Further *(and very important),* they should be sensitive to the move of the Holy Spirit within the service.

Psalms 33:2-3 "Give thanks to the LORD with the lyre; sing praises to Him with a harp of ten strings. Sing to Him a new song; Play skillfully with a shout of joy."

John 4:24 "God is spirit, and those who worship Him must worship in spirit and truth."

A wrong spontaneous action during this very delicate part of the service may bring the excitement of the revival down. It will also hinder the flow of the Holy Spirit and make it very difficult for the Evangelist to minister.

AN ORGANIZATIONAL MEETING SHOULD INCLUDE:

1. The appointment of a secretary who would be responsible for keeping records
2. Scheduling prayer meetings to pray for *the:*
    - Evangelistic town or city
    - People in the community
    - Church where the service is going to be held
    - Evangelist and their evangelistic team
    - Unsaved
    - Mighty out-pouring of the Holy Spirit
3. Announcements, printing, media campaigns and communication with local pastors and ministries to prepare the community for Revival

CONDUCTING A REVIVAL SERVICE

The Revival Service should be conducted with the utmost respect for God, the Holy Spirit and the Gospel.

THE SERMON

The sermon should meet the immediate needs of the church or community with much attention paid to the "Subject" and length of the sermon.

THE OFFERING

Taking the offering early in the service is suggested. It should not be forced nor should there be any form of "spiritual bribery." The suggestion that God would move in a particular manner based on an amount of money, should never be made by the Evangelist or the person taking the offering. The Spirit of God does not operate that way because you simply cannot pay for the Holy Spirit.

Acts 8:19-20 "And when Simon saw that through laying on of the apostles' hands the Holy Ghost was given, he offered them money, Saying, Give me also this power, that on whomsoever I lay hands, he may receive the Holy Ghost. But Peter said unto him, Thy money perish with thee, because thou hast thought that the gift of God may be purchased with money."

THE REVIVAL TEAM

Those who are part of the evangelistic team should be anointed, trained and experienced in Personal Evangelism and Soul Winning.

THE EMPOWERED

Those who are more experienced and demonstrate higher degrees of spirituality, *(including the Spiritual Gifts of Wisdom and Discerning of Spirits)* should the ones called upon to pray and work the altar.

REVIVAL SENTRIES

Sentries are members of the evangelist team who are seated throughout the congregation to pray for the service, control disturbances and quietly minister to individuals as the need arises. Doing this ensures that the service continues in an orderly way.

PRAISE AND WORSHIP LEADER

This team member must flow with the Evangelist and movement of the Holy Spirit in the service. Choice of songs should be appropriate for every portion of the service. Song lyrics should respond to and support what is being said as well as what is being done.

> *For Example:* A soft, heart stirring song would be more suitable for an altar call rather than a spirited praise song. Singing and music should never drown-out the speaker.

ALTAR CALL AND WORKERS

The altar call should be clear, simple and nonjudgmental. Nothing should be said or done to embarrass anyone. This is the time to have people respond to the evangelistic message, the move of the Holy Spirit and the sentiment of their hearts. Therefore, the altar call should be made with love for God's people and altar workers should be sensitive and prayerful.

POST REVIVAL MEETING

We can never predict the movement of the Spirit of God because all services are different. Therefore, organizational and prayer meetings should follow each service.

At these meetings:

- Thought and spiritual insight are exchanged

- Mistakes and hindrances are prayed about

- Unity is developed among the team members

- Satan's forces against the revival are rebuked

While talking to God, and with each other on one accord, the Holy Spirit is most likely to re-direct or confirm actions that are to be taken.

NOTES

NOTES

CHAPTER ELEVEN

INTRODUCTION TO HOMILETICS

<u>Definition:</u> *Homiletics* is from the Greek word *"Homilia"* which means conversation, talk or discourse; it is the acquired skill of writing sermons.

There are three important components of Homiletical Sermon writing that must be understood to ensure the successful use of this skill; they are *the:*

1. Spiritual nature of the person giving the sermon

2. Choice and interpretation of the text

3. Ability to use the choice of text

COMPONENT #1 – SPIRITUAL NATURE

Spiritual Nature and the anointing is what changes ordinary words into life changing truths. It significantly contributes to the move of the Holy Spirit on the hearts of the people so that they apply what they've learn to their lives. This is all the more reason why spending time fasting, praying and studying the Word of God is necessary.

2ⁿᵈ Peter 2:-7 "Grace and peace be multiplied to you in the knowledge of God and of Jesus our Lord; seeing that His divine power has granted to us everything pertaining to life and godliness, through the true knowledge of Him who called us by His own glory and excellence. For by these He has granted to us His precious and magnificent promises, so that by them you may become partakers of *the* divine nature, having escaped the corruption that is in the world by lust. Now for this very reason also, applying all diligence, in your faith supply moral excellence, and in *your* moral excellence, knowledge, and in *your* knowledge, self-control, and in *your* self-control, perseverance, and in *your* perseverance, godliness, and in *your* godliness, brotherly kindness, and in *your* brotherly kindness, love." New American Standard

This type of character is important for all ministers and teachers of God's Word, which is why they should take note of the *following:*

1. The most important characteristic of any speaker is humility. Audiences dislike arrogant and prideful speakers in any Christian Service.

2. Preaching or teaching God's word does not come easy. Therefore, seeking God for insight and interpretation of His Word should be a speaker's main commitment.

3. Speakers of God's Word must develop a sincere feeling of obligation to the duties of God's calling on their lives without compromise to any aspect of it.

4. God's Word is not intended to manipulate or confuse His people. As God's spokesperson, truthfulness and honesty is a mandate.

5. Inspiration comes from God and is used to infuse His message to bring it to life. An inspired teacher or preacher proves that the message is relatable and influential to those hearing it.

All of these characteristics are based upon living a Godly life. This is achieved *by:*

- Spending time with God in prayer and meditation

   Psalm 49:3 "My mouth shall speak of wisdom; and the meditation of my heart *shall be* of understanding."

- Presenting of *"self"* daily

   Romans 12:1 "I beseech you therefore, brethren, by the mercies of God, that ye present your bodies a living sacrifice, holy, acceptable unto God, *which is* your reasonable service."

- Study of the Word

   2nd Timothy 2:15 "Study to shew thyself approved unto God, a workman that needeth not to be ashamed, rightly dividing the word of truth."

COMPONENT #2 – CHOICE AND INTERPRETATION OF SCRIPTURE

Bible Context is a method used to find the meaning of passages of Scripture. There are four principles to this method of Bible *study:*

Principal Context – sheds light on a particular subject, thing or concept. In this principal, we must study the Scriptures that are before and after the subject matter.

Near Context – is applied to help clarify some of the hard to understand Scriptures by cross-referencing them with other Scriptures.

Remote Context – when a particular Scripture seems obscure or vague, to get clarity we may need to use Reference Books, Bible Dictionaries, Commentaries and other translations of our Bible.

Application of Context – after discovering its truth, the Scripture can then be applied, in some cases more than once. It is possible to have several applications, but there can only be one interpretation.

THE ABILITY TO USE SELECTED TEXT

The word *"text"* derives from the Latin *"textus" or "textrum."* It means *"something that is spun or woven."* Applying this to sermon writing, you should clearly understand your choice of "Text." Because the "Text" is the Biblical foundation of your "Subject," it should bring revelation, insight and illumination to your sermon.

Your ability to select and use the right "Text" in your sermon will change your life as well as the lives of the people in your audience. Being able to use your "Text" selection literally *(stating the facts "as is")* and figuratively *(being able to illustrate those facts using figures of speech, pictorials or examples)* will make a tremendous impact as well.

COMPONENT #3 – APPLICATION

The minister should be able to preach their sermon in a way that will have their audience respond *by:*

- Thinking carefully, about what is being said

- Sensing the anointing of God upon them as a result of the sermon

- Responding to the objective of the sermon

To have this happen the minister should always be mindful of what they *are:*

- *Doing* – Pride, flesh and ulterior motives must be put aside

- *Saying* – Must line-up with Scripture and their lifestyle

- *Handling* – The Word of God, His Law, Commandments, Statutes...which are Holy

NOTES

NOTES

INTRODUCTION TO HOMILETICS WORKSHEET

Your "Spiritual Nature" can be improved *by:*

1. Spending time with God in prayer and meditation
2. Presenting of *"self"* daily
3. Study of the Word

Match the following Scriptures with the statements *above:*

2ⁿᵈ Timothy 2:15 "Study to shew thyself approved unto God, a workman that needeth not to be ashamed, rightly dividing the word of truth."

1. [ ]   2. [ ]   3. [ ]

Psalm 49:3 "My mouth shall speak of wisdom; and the meditation of my heart *shall be* of understanding."

1. [ ]   2. [ ]   3. [ ]

Romans 12:1 "I beseech you therefore, brethren, by the mercies of God, that ye present your bodies a living sacrifice, holy, acceptable unto God, *which is* your reasonable service."

1. [ ]   2. [ ]   3. [ ]

Write your personal "Declaration" to improve your "Spiritual Nature" using these statements and Scriptures:

_____

_____

_____

_____

_____

CHAPTER TWELVE

FIVE SERMON WRITING STYLES

This chapter introduces five sermon models that *will:*

- Guide the minister in the delivery of a comprehensive and conclusive sermon

- Keep an audience interested in the sermon

- Ensure that the primary goal of the sermon to teach, encourage and inspire God's people is accomplished

FIVE SERMON MODELS

Word Outline – focuses on expounding specific words in a passage of Scripture

Phrase Outline – combines two passages of Scriptures for a conclusion that coincides with the "Subject" *(aim or topic)* of the sermon

Pictorial or Illustrative Outline – paints a picture or tells a story using the selected "Text" *(passage of Scripture)*

Textural or Investigative Outline – is a teaching method of sermonizing that answers the questions of "what, why, how and the results" of the sermon "Subject" *(aim or topic)*

Propositional Outline – Proves the objective of the "Subject" (*aim or topic)* of the sermon

All sermons must have the following Six components to achieve the homiletical results of sermon writing:

1. SALUTATION OR GREETING

Always give a greeting before you start. Your greeting should include *acknowledging:*

- The Pastor of the church
- Other ministers on the platform, those who are in your direct view in the audience and honored guests who were

mention by the officiator *(the person who governs the order and flow of the service)*

- Your guest or the people who came to support you

- The audience with warmth and sincerity

2. **A SUBJECT** – which is the aim or topic of the sermon

This should be a short statement of the core point of your sermon. It is what you want your audience to remember and apply to their lives.

3. **THE TEXT** – the passage of Scripture you use as a foundation for your sermon

- The "Text" must correspond with the "Subject" *(aim or topic)*

- Your "Text" *(passage of Scripture)* is the Biblical foundation that supports the "Subject" of your sermon. Therefore, it must correspond with your "Subject"
  Refer to The Ability to Use Selected Text on Page 108.

- Always research words you don't understand. Use an online audible dictionary to learn how to pronounce words and Biblical names

4. **INTRODUCTION TO THE SERMON** – this is the bridge that connects the "Subject" with the sermon

Seven Points to writing a solid Sermon Introduction:

1. Never make the "Introduction" too long

2. Make sure the "Introduction" relates to the "Subject"

3. If the "Text" necessitates clarification due to common misinterpretations, make them in the "Introduction"

4. Associate the "Introduction" with special themes and occasions

5. Make sure *that:*

✓ All of the facts, statistics and main character names are included and are correctly pronounced

✓ There is an ability to run the "Introduction" smoothly into the sermon

✓ You have a complete understanding of the "Text"

6. The "Introduction" should be presented in a way that portrays you as a trained and knowledgeable speaker

7. Writing out your "Introduction" is acceptable, especially if there are facts, statistics, comparisons of opinions, quotes or story-telling

5. THE SERMON – Four important points to remember:

1. Respect the allotted time-frame given for your sermon

2. Do not take liberties that where not extended to you *(ask for offerings, making altar calls, having people take oaths or make pledges, etc.)*

3. Self-control is one of the most important characteristics of any person giving an oral presentation of any kind

4. Never confess that you are nervous or show anxiousness *(you will lose the confidence of your audience)*

6. THE CONCLUSION

Summarize all of the key points of your sermon so that your audience will remember and respond to them.

NOTES

NOTES

THE WORD OUTLINE

Using this model of sermonizing, the speaker will use specific words from their "Text" to write their sermon. A general rule is to use a short passage of Scripture for this sermon style.

- ✓ GIVE THE SALUTATION

- ✓ STATE YOUR SUBJECT

- ✓ TEXT: Proverbs 3:5 "Trust in the Lord"

- ✓ INTRODUCTION TO SERMON

SERMON

First Word: Trust (expound the word *Trust*)

Second Word: In (expound the word *In*)

Third Word: Lord *(Teach the attributes, ability and willingness of the Lord to help us)*

THE CONCLUSION

Take all of the facts gathered from each Word *(in their correct order)* and bring them together in a summary. Close with a heart-felt statement that we must "Trust in the Lord."

NOTES

NOTES

THE WORD OUTLINE WORKSHEET

SALUTATION

_____

_____

SUBJECT

_____

_____

_____

TEXT

_____

INTRODUCTION TO SERMON

_____

_____

_____

_____

SERMON

FIRST WORD

_____

_____

_____

_____

SECOND WORD

_____

_____

_____

Third Word

The Conclusion

THE PHRASE OUTLINE

Words within a particular passage of Scripture are used as the foundation for structuring a sermon using the Phrase Outline. You may use a group of words within one passage or take phrases from other passages of Scripture and combine them to make this outline.

When combining phrases from different Scriptures, make sure that they coincide with each other and the "Subject" to make a fluent outline.

For Example: Phrase *(the scripture you are using)* #1: *Matthew 7:7 "Ask, and it shall be given you; seek, and ye shall find; knock, and it shall be opened unto you."* Combined with Phrase *(the scripture you are using)* #2: *Revelation 3:8 "I know thy works: behold, I have set before thee an open door, and no man can shut it: for thou hast a little strength, and hast kept my word, and hast not denied my name."*

- ✓ GIVE THE SALUTATION

- ✓ STATE YOUR SUBJECT *(from these two passages of scriptures, your subject should relate to seeking God for an opportunity or His favor)*

- ✓ THE TEXT – Let your audience know that you are combining both passages of Scriptures. *(It is appropriate to read each phrase)*

- ✓ INTRODUCTION TO SERMON

THE SERMON

Phrase #1: *(the scripture you are using)*
Matthew 7:7 "Ask, and it shall be given you; seek, and ye shall find; knock, and it shall be opened unto you."

Give 3 – 4 key observations about this passage of Scripture.

Phrase #2: *(the second scripture you are using)*

Revelation 3:8 "I know thy works: behold, I have set before thee an open door, and no man can shut it: for thou hast a little strength, and hast kept my word, and hast not denied my name."

Give 3 – 4 key observations about this passage of Scripture in combination with the previous.

THE CONCLUSION

Take all of the facts gathered from the combination of both Scriptures and bring them together in a summary that relates to your "Subject."

NOTES

NOTES

THE PHRASE OUTLINE WORKSHEET

SALUTATION

_____

_____

SUBJECT

_____

_____

_____

TEXT *(let your audience know that you are combining both passages of Scriptures. It is appropriate to read each phrase)*

#1 _____   #2_____

INTRODUCTION TO SERMON

_____

_____

_____

_____

SERMON:

Phrase #1: "Text" *(the scripture you are using)*

✓ Discuss 3 – 4 key observations about this passage of Scripture.

  1: _____

2: _____

3: _____

4: _____

Phrase #2: "Text" *(the second scripture you are using)*

   ✓ Give 3 – 4 key observations about this passage of Scripture in combination with the previous.

     1: _____

     2: _____

     3: _____

     4: _____

THE CONCLUSION

Take all of the facts gathered from the combination of both Scriptures and bring them together in a summary that relates to your "Subject."

_____

_____

_____

_____

_____

_____

_____

_____

_____

THE PICTORIAL OUTLINE

The Pictorial Outline is an illustrative style of sermonizing which gives the audience a visual of the "Text." The "Subject," "Introduction" and "Conclusion" must coincide with the "Text" that is being illustrated.

STEPS TO ILLUSTRATING A PICTORIAL OR ILLUSTRATIVE SERMON:

1. GIVE THE SALUTATION

2. THE SUBJECT *(what you visualize)*

3. THE TEXT *(the Scripture you are using)* to paint your picture or basis for your story

4. THE INTRODUCTION would be the model or visual idea of what you are going to paint

   For example: If you wanted to paint a flower, you would look at one very carefully so that you would be able to sketch it. Your "Introduction" is what you'll use to begin your illustration

5. THE SERMON – Paint your picture through your sermon

6. THE CONCLUSION is the finished picture

NOTES

NOTES

THE PICTORIAL/ILLUSTRATIVE OUTLINE WORKSHEET

SALUTATION

_____

_____

SUBJECT *(what you visualize)*

_____

_____

_____

TEXT *(the Scripture you are using)* to paint your picture or basis for your story)

_____

INTRODUCTION (the visual idea of what you are going to paint)

_____

_____

_____

_____

THE SERMON *(paint your picture through your sermon)*

_____

_____

_____

_____

_____

_____

_____

_____

_____

_____

_____

_____

_____

_____

THE CONCLUSION *(the finished picture)*

_____

_____

_____

_____

_____

_____

_____

_____

_____

_____

_____

_____

_____

_____

THE PROPOSITIONAL OUTLINE

The Propositional style of sermonizing sets out to prove or detail the statement of the "Subject" *(aim or topic)* of your sermon.

Definition: *Proposition* (1) anything stated for the purposes of discussion (2) logic, a statement affirming or denying something so that it can be characterized as true or false.

- ✓ GIVE YOUR SALUTATION

- ✓ STATE YOUR SUBJECT: "Nothing is too hard for God"

- ✓ TEXT (choose one that gives an example related to your "Subject")

- ✓ INTRODUCTION
  1. Speak about the conditions of society today

  2. At the end of the "Introduction" ask this question "Is there anything too hard for God *(this question is your Proposition)*?" You will prove through your sermon, that there is nothing too hard for God.

SERMON

List at least FIVE strong proofs that there is nothing too hard for God.

Support each proof with a Scripture that gives an example of how God changes situations and struggles in the lives of His people.

THE CONCLUSION

Because you have proven the point of your "Subject" *("Nothing is too hard for God")* in your sermon, there is no need to restate facts or make a summary; you would simply repeat your "Subject." Or, ask the question, "Is there anything too hard for God?"

Answer the question with "No", there is nothing too hard for God!" Appeal to your audience to trust God with their issue.

NOTES

THE PROPOSITIONAL OUTLINE WORKSHEET

SALUTATION

_____

_____

SUBJECT

_____

_____

_____

TEXT (choose one that give an example related to your "Subject")

_____

INTRODUCTION TO SERMON (make a bold intriguing statement that you intend to prove in your sermon)

_____

_____

_____

_____

SERMON (prove your introduction statement with supporting scriptures)

_____

_____

_____

_____

_____

_____

_____

_____

_____

_____

_____

_____

_____

_____

_____

THE CONCLUSION (repeat your "Subject" in a way that shows that you have proven it's point)

_____

_____

_____

_____

_____

_____

_____

_____

_____

_____

_____

_____

_____

_____

_____

THE INVESTIGATIVE OR EXPLORATORY OUTLINE

Using the Investigative method of sermonizing, the "Subject" of the sermon is analyzed by answering four basic questions: *what, why, how, results.* Doing this gives the audience a complete understanding of the "Subject."

This outline is perfect for ministers who are teachers of the Word. It can also be used to format personal Bible Study, reports, speeches and proposals.

THE FOUR BASIC QUESTIONS:

1. What *(an examination of what is being discussed)*

2. Why *(the importance of what is being discussed)*

3. How *(the procedures used)*

4. Results *(the end results)*

    ✓ GIVE YOUR SALUTATION

    ✓ STATE YOUR SUBJECT: The Resurrection of Christ

    ✓ TEXT *(related to the Resurrection of Jesus Christ)*

    ✓ INTRODUCTION *(should be similar to the style of the Propositional Outline Introduction)*

SERMON

It is Easter Sunday, and you are going to investigate important facts pertaining to the Resurrection of Christ's through your sermon. You will ask and answer *the:*

"WHAT" of Christ's Resurrection

- His purpose for coming *(Scriptures)*

- The Father's Will *(Scriptures)*

The significance of death by crucifixion *(Scriptures)*

"WHY" or the "Importance" of Christ's Resurrection as it *relates to:*

- Mankind's freedom from sin *(Scriptures)*
- God's provision of Salvation *(Scriptures)*
- Satan's influence and hold on mankind *(Scriptures)*

"HOW" of Christ's Resurrection

- Jesus' promise that He will rise *(Scriptures)*
- The involvement of the Holy Spirit *(Scriptures)*
- The angels at the tomb *(Scriptures)*

"RESULTS" of Christ's Resurrection as it relates *to:*

- Mankind *(Scriptures)*
- Christ's Glory and heavenly Priesthood *(Scriptures)*
- Descending of the Holy Spirit *(Scriptures)*
- Benefiting the Church *(Scriptures)*

THE CONCLUSION

Summarize all of the key points of your Sermon so that your audience will remember and respond to it.

NOTES

NOTES

THE INVESTIGATIVE OR EXPLORATORY OUTLINE WORKSHEET

SALUTATION

_____

_____

SUBJECT

_____

_____

_____

TEXT *(must relate to you "Subject")*

_____

INTRODUCTION *(should be similar to the style of the Propositional Outline Introduction)*

_____

_____

_____

_____

SERMON

Teach important facts pertaining to the "Subject" with 2-3 supporting Scriptures)

"WHAT" *(give an explanation of your "Subject")*

1. _____ *Scripture:*_____

2. _____ *Scripture:*_____

3. _____ *Scripture:*_____

"WHY" *(explain the importance of your investigation of the "Subject")*

1. _____ *Scripture:*_____
2. _____ *Scripture:*_____
3. _____ *Scripture:*_____

"HOW" *(explain various ways or procedures related to your "Subject")*

1. _____ *Scripture:*_____
2. _____ *Scripture:*_____
3. _____ *Scripture:*_____

"RESULTS" *(what where the final results of your investigation of your "Subject")*

1. _____ *Scripture:*_____
2. _____ *Scripture:*_____
3. _____ *Scripture:*_____

THE CONCLUSION

Summarize all of the key points of your Sermon so that your audience will remember and respond to it.

_____

_____

_____

_____

_____

To Learn More about the Bible order THE INTRODUCTION SERIES:

INTRODUCTION TO BIBLE DOCTRINE
*A Systematic Study of Seven Doctrines of the Christian Faith –
Made Easy*

INTRODUCTION TO BIBLE ORIGIN
A Study of the Formation of the Bible

INTRODUCTION TO TYPOLOGY AND SYMBOLISM
An Expository Study of Types and Symbols Found in the Bible

To Receive a Certificate in Biblical Studies in five short months:
Go to: **www.theinstituteoftheology.org**

Devotional Studies to Empower Your Spiritual:

WHEN YOU PRAY ... PRAY LIKE THIS
All you need to know about Prayer

THE SECRET PLACE OF THE MOST HIGH ... *How to Get There*

All available at Amazon.com *(by title)*

or

Visit: www.swalkerpublications.com

www.ingramcontent.com/pod-product-compliance
Lightning Source LLC
Chambersburg PA
CBHW071758090426
42737CB00012B/1871